Wheels Around Dundee

by
Alan Brotchie and Jack Herd

One-horse carts of this style were quite a common sight until after the Second World War. They were used for a multitude of tasks, from transporting produce to market to removing dung from the streets (ideally not in the same cart). This photograph was taken in Dudhope Street, near the Hilltown. Number 40, behind the cart, was home to Tanbini's Fish Restaurant, here advertising its fish suppers, iced drinks and 'clean cooking'. Number 38 on the left was Mrs McLaren's confectionery and smallware establishment (what qualified as 'smallware'?).

© Alan Brotchie 2002
First published in the United Kingdom, 2002,
Reprinted 2007
by Stenlake Publishing Limited
Telephone / Fax: 01290 551122

ISBN 9781840332100

Right: For many years the classical facade of the old Coffee House and Assembly Rooms formed the eastern boundary of the Greenmarket, the focus of fairs and markets. Today it is one of the few remaining Georgian buildings in the city centre. In the foreground horses drink from a granite water trough, several of which were to be found throughout the city. In many centres of industry such troughs were donated by kind-hearted citizens for the benefit of hard-working horses.

Left: The title on this old lantern slide merely reads 'Gutter Merchants', but a little detective work has uncovered that the delightful Victorian scene is of two fishwives - probably from Broughty Ferry - selling their wares outside the Crown Bar on Shore Terrace facing the Greenmarket in Dundee city centre. (This original Shore Terrace was at right angles to the later one at the rear of the Caird Hall and faced the foot of Crichton Street.) The Crown Hotel above the bar of the same name (denoted by the lamp above its door) was owned by a Mrs Steel in the early years of the last century, who would have had to rule such a busy dockside establishment with a rod of iron.

Opposite: Fred Coutts was personal assistant – and later engineer – to the Dundee & District Tramway Co. Ltd. A former pupil of Morgan Academy, such was his consuming interest in tramways that he initially worked without remuneration! For their summer holidays, he and his family were wont to hire one of the company's horse buses to explore their native Scotland. Bus number 30, which was normally to be found plying to and from Downfield, is seen here with the Coutts family at Birkie Brae, near the entrance to Camperdown Estate by Lochee in 1897. On this occasion the trip was to include Killin, Aberfeldy, Comrie and St Fillans – all visited at a leisurely pace. Coutts, who was a keen amateur photographer, left Dundee in 1901 to become manager of Ayr Corporation Tramways, then transferred in 1905 to the much larger Paisley District Tramways. When that undertaking was acquired by Glasgow Corporation in August 1923, he took up the final post of his career as manager of the Dearne District Tramways in Yorkshire.

INTRODUCTION

Dundee's privileged situation on the south-facing northern shore of the River Tay has, since the time of the earliest recorded Royal Charter in the twelfth century, ensured that growth has developed around its natural harbour and strategic position. King William the Lion created the small settlement as a Royal Burgh in 1190, the century which saw the foundation of St Mary's Church – the earliest component of the Town's Churches building which still remains in the centre of the city conurbation.

As a strategic centre the growing settlement attracted the unwelcome attention of marauding English armies who torched the area with almost monotonous regularity, commencing with the army of Edward I in 1303 and followed by those of Edward III in 1335, the Duke of Somerset in 1547 and the Marquis of Montrose in 1645. Finally in 1651 the town was besieged by General Monck on behalf of Oliver Cromwell. After this last event matters settled down and the community was left to grow and prosper through the ensuing centuries up to the time of the Industrial Revolution. However, it was only in the Victorian era that the city commenced its first

major expansion beyond the medieval limits which had, until then, formed the extent of the populated area. This period saw the population grow from 45,355 at the time of the census of 1831 to 140,063 by the census 50 years later in 1881. Growth after this time continued at a lesser rate.

Dundee was an early centre of railway development in Scotland with its first railway, the line to Newtyle, opening in 1831–32, to be followed on 6 October 1838 by a line linking the town with Arbroath. The latter line, and the contemporary Arbroath & Forfar Railway, were built to the 'Scottish Standard' gauge of 5 ft 6 ins, and at the Parliamentary Inquiry for the determination of a 'Standard' or 'Parliamentary' gauge for the whole nation this wider gauge was stoutly defended by the railways' respective engineers. The Dundee & Newtyle, however, had been built to another gauge of 4 ft 6 ins. Ultimately all had to give way and were rebuilt to the stipulated 4 ft 8½ ins which prevailed virtually everywhere within the United Kingdom. A line – to 4 ft 8½ ins gauge this time – was opened to Perth in 1847. This fledgling railway activity also spawned a short-lived local locomotive engine construction industry.

Dundee is a hilly city (it was awarded city status in 1889) and local public transport was inaugurated several years after other Scottish cities had built tramway systems. Dundee's first tram line opened in 1877 and after a very few years it was found that the cost of operation by horses on the hilly streets was uneconomic. Small steam engines hauling much larger trams were the answer, and Dundee ultimately had the largest operation of this type in Scotland. Electric trams appeared in 1900, but the last steam tram lumbered on for a further two years. (One of Dundee's steam trams can be seen at the National Tramway Museum at Crich in Derbyshire.) Dundee's electric trams were very successful in the compact city and served the populace well – and profitably – until 1956. Buses were early on the scene, and it has been possible to illustrate the very first of these.

Gathering the old photographs used to illustrate *Wheels Around Dundee* has been underway for many years, since I lived in Dundee over 30 years ago. Those selected represent just the 'tip of the iceberg'. Dundee seems to have had a disproportionately large number of early photographic enthusiasts, both professional and amateur, and to them must go the thanks of all social historians. Of particular assistance have been Messrs D. C. Thomson Ltd., Robert Grieves and Dundee Libraries.

Jack Herd my friend for nearly 40 years and collaborator on several 'Old Dundee' books, died on 2 May 2002, prior to completion of this work.

A. W. Brotchie
June 2002.

No book of this nature dealing with Dundee could possibly ignore the tragedy of the collapse of the first Tay railway bridge in the ferocious gale late on the night of 28 December 1879. This view was probably taken just prior to the official opening of the bridge in May of the previous year, and gives a graphic indication of the slenderness of the structure. The small locomotive in the centre is probably the four-wheeled 'pug' owned by the contractors who built the bridge, Hopkins, Gilkes & Co. of Middlesborough. The deck-level triangular 'fillets', examples of which are seen in front of the locomotive, may have paid a significant part in the catastrophe, as it is possible that when the derailed train hit one of them it was thrown against the downstream face of the high girders. This impact would have added to the effect of the hurricane-force winds, dealing a blow which the structure could not withstand.

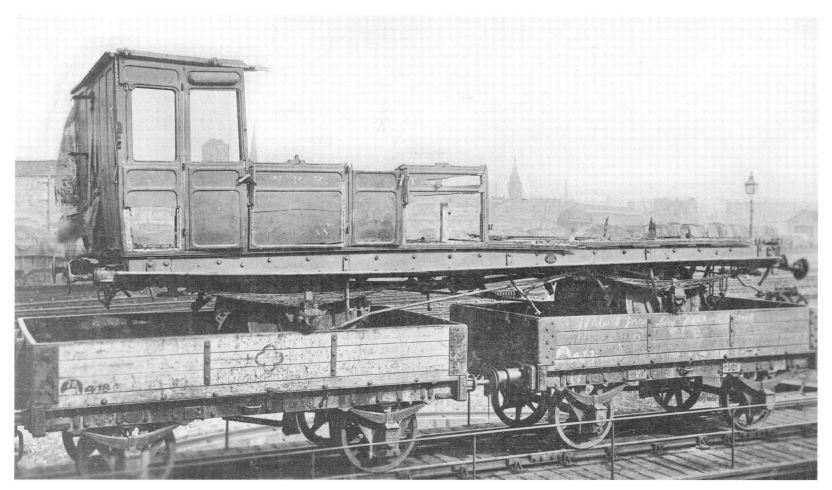

Reproduced from a postcard entitled 'Old Tay Bridge disaster, 1879, one of the carriages', this image shows the remains of one of the three third class carriages which formed part of the doomed train. The photograph was taken in the railway yards of Dundee West station. Many views of the remains of the bridge were produced after the traumatic event, and local postcard manufacturers later sold sets of these in large numbers. The originator of this particular example is not identified on the card, but is thought to be the pioneer Dundee photographer, James Valentine. Photographs of the tickets collected from passengers at St Fort station, the last stop in Fife before the train ventured onto the bridge, reveal that very few first class passengers were on board, with most of those remaining on the train (some 75) being in the third class carriages. Many souvenirs were made and sold from the wooden remains of the carriages including walking sticks and money boxes.

This fine Victorian still-life study is entitled 'Old Catholic Church, Eagles Close, Dundee' and is dated November 1895. Eagles Close was at 108 Murraygate. Note that the two hansom cabs are of considerably differing design. That closest to the camera is owned by James Brown while the other has its licence number, nine, clearly painted on the drivers 'perch'. Dundee's official Hackney carriage licence conditions stated that the fare could be withheld by the hirer if the name of the owner and the number were not painted on the outside. When this photograph was taken a typical fare from High Street to Stobswell was one shilling, a lot of money compared to the tram fare of only one penny. Here the old church has been given over to secular use – note the open window with lifting beam above to heave in hay and foodstuff for the horses stabled there.

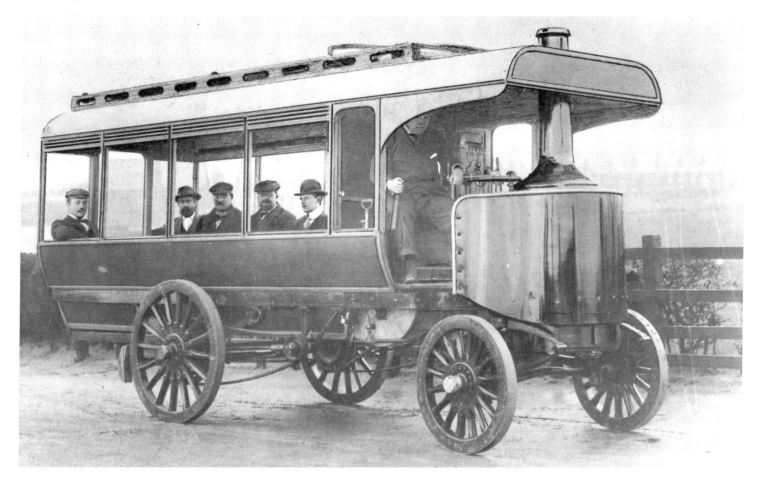

Dundee's privately-owned tramway company showed that it was at the forefront of modern thinking when, with its tramways about to be taken over by the Corporation, it obtained this pioneering Leyland steam bus in May 1899. It had previously been exhibited at a motor show in Edinburgh, albeit in an incomplete state, and was thereafter driven under its own power to the city, meeting curious spectators all along its route. As soon as it arrived it was placed in service running from Fairmuir to Downfield. It is not known how long it lasted, its departure being rather less well publicised than its arrival! The solid wheels were very unforgiving on the water-bound macadam roads of the day which turned into dust bowls in the summer and mud baths in winter. The 20-seat body was entered by a step at the rear, and the vehicle could also be operated as an open charabanc. Its purchase was factored by John Stirling of Hamilton, a pioneer of Scottish motoring who is said to have operated the first motorised passenger service in Britain. This bus was a first too, credited with being Dundee's first 'horseless carriage'.

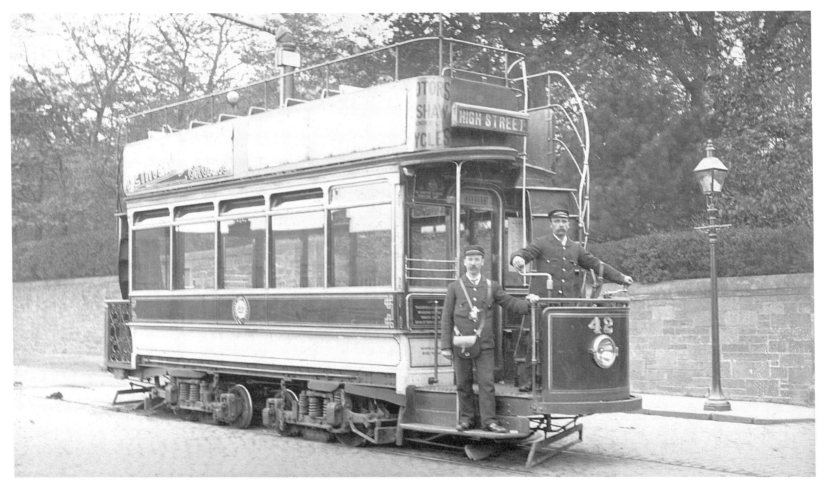

When Dundee's electric trams commenced operation at the beginning of the twentieth century, all of the first 48 cars were open-topped, like car 42, which was photographed at Lochee terminus with its proud driver and conductor. Of these first trams eighteen were of this style – on eight wheels – while the remainder ran on four-wheeled trucks. The eighteen bogie cars were initially thought more suitable for Dundee's hilly routes. A top deck cover, to give weather protection to the upper deck passengers, was added in 1906–07. Dundonians did not take favourably to the open top – even the outdated steam trams which preceded these had the top deck enclosed, and a fine fug could be generated therein! In 1927 this particular specimen was renumbered 12 and became the guinea-pig for the modernisation of most of the Dundee tram fleet. However, it was not until 1930 that it finally assumed the same form as its contemporaries.

This is the same tram as seen in the previous picture after 50-plus years of service on Dundee's streets. All of the original eighteen eight-wheeled vehicles were rebuilt to end up looking like this – fully enclosed on both decks, fitted with the latest up-to-date electrical equipment and smartly painted. The reconstruction work was carried out in the Corporation Transport Department's workshops in Lochee Road. This type, with five windows to the saloon, ran mostly on the Blackness to Downfield route until its closure 'as an experiment' on 26 November 1955 (was it really so long ago?). At that date the oldest cars running were two years older than even this veteran, but looked just the same as it. Dundee's trams all had a similar appearance and usually looked very smart in their leaf green and white colours. Many of the drivers and conductors were amongst the elite band of Dundee 'characters' – how many remember the singing driver Willie Grindle, his speciality the old Scots songs? Car 12 (the former 42) was photographed in Blackness Road by Glaswegian tram enthusiast Bob Clark in its final year of operation.

A stunning portrait of Dundee tram 27 posed in the High Street, looking west with the distinctive turreted corner building known as General Monck's Lodging immediately behind it. This was one of the many historic structures which were a feature of the city centre until the middle of last century when much needed 'improvement' removed not just slums but buildings of distinction also. To the left of the tram is the continuation of High Street into the Nethergate, whilst on the right can be seen the commencement of the Overgate, which with Seagate, Cowgate, Murraygate and Wellgate formed medieval entrances to the burgh. This particular tram is of interest as it was the first to receive this distinctive top deck cover which, while enclosing the centre area, left the ends – which smokers were encouraged to frequent – open to the elements!

A rare off-route trip for this single-deck 'Constitution Road' type tramcar. Having been removed from its normal terminus at the south end of Reform Street, a temporary reversal point in Meadowside opposite the Albert Institute was set up while the track and point work on the usual route was renewed. Detail of how the tram track was constructed is well illustrated here, with the 'girder' rails laid on a layer of reinforced concrete and tie rods used to hold the rails on the curve at the correct gauge. Also note the conductor of the tram who is using a long bamboo pole to assist in guiding the trolley through the maze of overhead wires.

There has been considerable recent press debate regarding the old motor vehicle registration letters for Dundee – TS – postulating that they were initially given to Mr Tom Shaw in gratitude by a friend of his who was receiving driving lessons and who was behind the derivation of the letter scheme. The basis of the scheme was, however, a logical allocation of letters following an alphabetical listing first of the counties, then of the cities and towns authorised to register vehicles after January 1904. Dundee thus fell after Aberdeen (RS) and before Govan (US) in the latter series (SS – for ▶

◀ Haddingtonshire – had been used up in the county series where 'S' formed the first letter of the pair). TS 1, when first issued, was allocated to Mr Alexander Watt (the well-known photographer with premises at 30 Reform Street) whose home then was Primus Villa, Arbroath Road. Seen there are TS 1 – an 8 hp De Dion Bouton (possibly the 1903 model) which was painted dark green – and its one horsepower predecessor. To return to the story, Tom Shaw was one of Dundee's first local motorists and became a leader in the motor trade, joining the Scottish Motor Trade Association and exhibiting at the 1904 Edinburgh Motor Show. Perhaps he capitalised on the TS coincidence!

For a short period, from 1907 to 1910, Dundee had its own motorcar construction industry when brothers William and Edward Raikes Bell created the 'Werbell' car, of which this is an example. They owned premises in Ward Road, where the telegraphic address was 'Horseless, Dundee'. Only a few Werbells were constructed and all, so far as is known, used engines supplied by White & Poppel. The emergent motorcar industry spawned a remarkable number of manufacturers, many of whom disappeared quickly having made little or no impact on the market. Some, however, became forces to be reckoned with, and the marques remembered by Scottish automotive historians include the Kelvin and St Vincent of Glasgow, the Dalhousie from Carnoustie and the St Laurence, built in Laurencekirk – not to mention the more successful and therefore longer-lasting Argyll and Arrol Johnston.

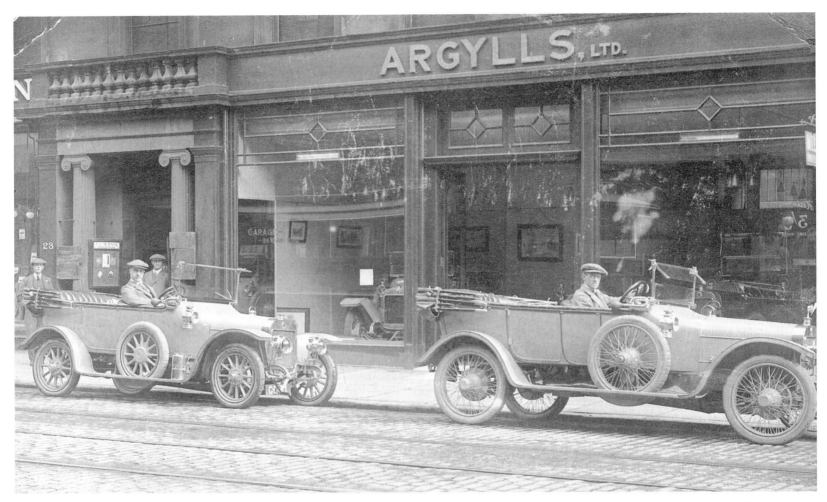

The showroom of Messrs Argylls at 17 Reform Street, photographed *c*.1914. Three of their cars can be seen in the picture, including one in the showroom window. Their local manager, Mr Mohr (right), is driving the 15/30 hp model with wire wheels, while behind is an example of the 12/18 hp model, this one with wooden wheels. That in the showroom is the 25/50 hp model. Manufactured in Alexandria, Dunbartonshire from 1899 until 1914, this view must have been taken not long before production ceased. The overstated and grandiose facade of the factory in Alexandria, complete with carvings in stone of emerging cars, can be seen to this day, although it now forms part of the frontage of a series of factory outlet shops, and – more appropriately – a small motor museum.

During the 1920s the Chief Medical Officer of Health was Mr William Burgess, and it is thought that this scene shows him on his rounds in his handsome, if rather elderly, chauffeur-driven Renault limousine. Note that unusually its radiator is behind the bonnet. The contrast between the old Victorian housing on the right and the new construction dating from the immediate post First World War era (left) is marked. The scene is in the Stirling Park area, in Macaulay Street

Posing for a photograph on Dundee's Esplanade alongside the River Tay (now of course Riverside Drive) would not be recommended today. However in May 1910 when this new 28 hp Halley was its owner's pride and joy, the volume of traffic posed no safety problem. At the time TS 423 had been newly purchased by the Forfarshire Motor Bus Co. and must have looked most elegant in its dove grey enamel, tastefully and delicately lined out in dark blue. The company was formed by William Raikes Bell, who could perhaps be the bowler-hatted gentleman standing proudly beside his new purchase. Note the leather-covered bench seats and the bulb horn to the driver's right hand. Opened in 1875, the Esplanade is no longer a muddy track on the periphery of the city.

This was possibly one of TS 423's first outings as it still seems to have a pristine air, with not a speck of dust to sully its sides. Note its licence number '48' below the registration number on the rear panel. The bus in front is probably another Halley (possibly TS 375), but unfortunately neither it nor the occasion can be identified. The two vehicles appear to be attracting considerable attention, with one of G. L. Wilson's employees observing the scene from a first floor window, in addition to the interest being shown at ground level. The photograph was taken in Commercial Street at Wilson's corner. The massive architecture of Commercial Street was designed, surprisingly, by an engineer, not an architect. *Builder* magazine was critical: 'We understand the Burgh Engineer is responsible for the design . . . every one who is capable of judging architectural design must regret that a man who is probably exceptionally capable (he would hardly be Burgh Engineer if he were not) should have committed such an error of judgement'. Strong words indeed.

Passing through Muirhead on its way to Birkhill is the original 'horseless' Birkie bus – XS 178 – a 20-seat Arrol Johnston which had the distinction of being the first petrol-driven public service vehicle to be licensed by Dundee Magistrates – on 26 May 1909. The fare was fourpence single – a not inconsiderable sum when two shillings was a reasonable day's wage. The vehicle was provided with a removable roof and canvas side screens which gave passengers some protection in inclement weather. The sender of this postcard (on 26 July 1909) wrote 'Arrived all safe after an awful journey – were drowned . . . just as if we had been dragged along the road'. The joys of pioneer motoring!

This photograph shows the Liff bus about to depart from the stance in Lochee High Street with, in the right background, the old East United Free Church on the corner of Methven Street. This was later occupied as a shop by F. W. Woolworth. TS 363, a 14-seat 18/20 hp Halley, was known locally as 'the Boat' and was only the second motorbus to be licenced by Dundee's magistrates. Painted dark green, it was purchased new and first registered on 11 June 1909 under the ownership of Betsy Martin (or Cumming) of Lochee. The picture was probably taken soon afterwards. Note the horse-drawn brake behind ready to take any overflow passengers. The stance was in front of Hunt's butcher shop, and the figure in the traditional butcher's striped apron is perhaps James Hunt himself. Note also on the lamppost the sign advising (pedestrians!) to keep right. When a shift ended at Cox's Camperdown Works the tide of humanity could sweep all before it!

A. W. Watson of Fairmuir Garage in Strathmartine Road purchased this very smart 14-seat 20/36 hp Albion coach in April 1929. Registered TS 7961, it was painted cream with maroon upper work and had a removable hood which gave it a 'charabanc' feel on summer days. It was last recorded working on the Isle of Skye. The company ran their first tours in 1920 and by the forties were offering a comprehensive selection of holidays by bus of up to seven days' duration, mostly around the beauty-spots of Scotland, but also venturing as far away as the Lake District in that foreign country – England! These holidays were extremely popular in the post-war years before the allure of package deals to the Costas of Spain achieved mass appeal.

This area has changed radically since the photograph was taken just before the First World War, with only Union Street and Whitehall Crescent in the distance remaining recognisable. On the left is the former West station terminus, a fine example of railway company indulgence prevailing over economy, and built no doubt to literally overshadow the much busier NBR Tay Bridge in its depressing cutting just to the south. In the foreground is the Caledonian Railway carting department office, with a double-yoked horse cart taking advantage of the smooth path offered by the tramlines. It was no coincidence that the steel-shod wooden cartwheels neatly fitted the tram tracks, much to the annoyance of the tramway officials, particularly when the carter turned a deaf ear to the ringing of the tram's bell to get him to move over. Here the tramcar is running from Craig Pier to Baxter Park, the Craig Pier end of which route was abandoned as early as June 1919 – although vestiges of the rails were still to be found in 1961.

SOUTH UNION STREET, DUNDEE

Not every city had a railway locomotive named after it, but North British Railway No. 869, built in 1906, was called *Dundonian* and worked for most of its existence from that city's depot. One of 22 of this type, it was regularly used on express workings to Edinburgh or Aberdeen. Its companions at Dundee's loco depot were *Aberdonian*, *Highland Chief* and *Duke of Rothesay*. The North British had a way with names and made a point of giving their bronze green locomotives a patriotic theme. However, for some unfathomable reason *Dundonian* was renamed *Bonnie Dundee* in 1912, and as most people are aware this is not a reference to the city, but to Viscount Dundee, John Graham of Claverhouse, and was thus a rather less appropriate name. She was withdrawn from service in 1935 but another one of the type was later retained for preservation. Unfortunately in 1939 this last remaining example, *Midlothian*, was broken up for scrap.

Looking east along Dock Street from the junction with Trades Lane (left). Two horse-drawn carts are in view, the first with bales of jute (generally jute carts were very much more heavily laden than this). The horse hitched to the second cart has either been startled by the passing locomotive, or is attempting to give it a race! In the distance is the old East station of the Dundee & Arbroath Joint Railway (owned by the Caledonian and North British Railways) which closed at the beginning of January 1959. The imposing Ionic portico of the Custom House building, one of Scotland's largest, dates from 1843 and was erected at a cost of only £8,000. The small 'pug' locomotive in the centre belonged, unusually, to the Caledonian Railway. More frequently the harbour pugs – which had to conform to Harbour Board regulations including having a spark arrestor fitted on the chimney – were from the North British Railway. The Custom House now has a less imposing setting with the Tay Road Bridge approach roads on its doorstep.

Morning, noon and night saw the East station busy with commuters travelling from – and to – Broughty Ferry, Monifieth and beyond. Many city centre office workers even returned home for lunch. Recorded here are the crowds from the 2.23 p.m. arrival which had left from Barnhill at 2.05, Broughty Ferry at 2.10 and West Ferry at 2.12 p.m. (today's 'Sprinters' generally appear to be allowed eight to twelve minutes for the Broughty Ferry to Tay Bridge Station run). Note the hopeful horse cabs lined-up – not getting much custom from these regulars – and the large number of horse carts on the right (at least twenty can be counted). This area of former warehouses is being transformed by owners Forth Ports PLC in a £30 million-plus redevelopment of the Victoria and Camperdown Docks. The old jute storage sheds on the right are enjoying a new lease of life as the City Quay factory outlet shopping development, while a new 200-bedroom hotel is also under construction.

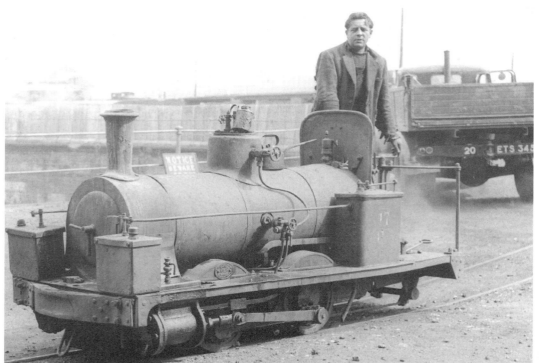

Dundee's own miniature railway! This 24-inch gauge line was used in the East Dock Street gasworks for the removal of coke and ashes. Despite its short length – just a third of a mile – it boasted no fewer than four of these diminutive locomotives. Supplied by Messrs Kerr, Stuart & Co. Ltd. of Stoke-on-Trent, the first two arrived in 1900 with the second pair delivered the following year. Originally carrying numbers 1–4, they were later renumbered 14–17 for some unfathomable reason. When the line became disused in 1959, such was their appeal that two of the four were rescued for preservation. No. 17, seen here, was not one of the lucky ones, but No. 16 went to the Narrow Gauge Railway Museum at Towyn in North Wales. No. 15 was purchased by steam enthusiast the late Ian N. Fraser of Arbroath and can now be found – considerably rebuilt, running as (a second) *Bonnie Dundee* on the Ravenglass & Eskdale Railway in the Lake District. This fascinating scene was photographed by Bernard Mettam in May 1956.

Magdalene Green, one of Dundee's smallest railway stations, was much used for events in the adjacent Riverside Park. This is former Caledonian Railway 0-6-0 locomotive 715, which had become LMS 17397 by the time the photograph was taken on 24 August 1928. It is seen here arriving on the 10.00 a.m. service from Perth, which stopped at all stations and took no less than 55 minutes to complete the 22-mile journey. Today 21 minutes are allowed – albeit non-stop. To the right of the locomotive the station name can be seen carefully delineated in whitewashed pebbles, the job no doubt carried out under the supervision of porter-in-charge Francis Fraser.

Looking from Magdalene Green station footbridge on the occasion of the Royal Highland and Agricultural Society's annual show in the summer of 1933. Prior to the society adopting its present permanent showground at Ingliston outside Edinburgh, the show was held in a different location each year, an arrangement which appealed to many in the agricultural community. A large selection of visitors' cars is on view, although very few exhibit Scottish registration marks. In the distance is a Corporation bus on a special service from the city centre, while further off a train from north Fife approaches the curved spans of the Tay Railway Bridge. Above and behind the station name board can be seen the 'Coupers' swimming pool, which was built in 1848 and used water straight from the nearby River Tay. At first glance it seems a most inhospitable spot in which to bathe – completely open to the elements and with no apparent redeeming features. Nevertheless it was highly popular and much missed after 1947 when it was filled in.

The famous Royal Arch at Shore Terrace on Dock Street. The original – of wood – was erected on this spot in 1844 to commemorate the visit of Queen Victoria and Prince Albert during that year. That temporary structure was replaced by this 80-foot high stone extravaganza – fondly known to locals as the 'Pigeon's Palace'! The architect, John T. Rochead of Glasgow, also designed the Wallace Monument at Causewayhead near Stirling. Like it or loathe it, it was yet another element of Dundee's heritage until like many other landmarks it was dismantled stone by stone in March 1964 and used to fill in the adjacent dock to form the landfall area for the Tay Road Bridge. Also to be seen is the old Empress Ballroom which had originally seen use at the Glasgow Empire Exhibition of 1938 and was afterwards re-erected on Dock Street. Saddle-tank locomotive 68107 is making its way (at 4 mph) with wagonloads of sand, possibly from the Tay Sand & Gravel Company's wharf in Earl Grey Dock on the extreme right of the photograph.

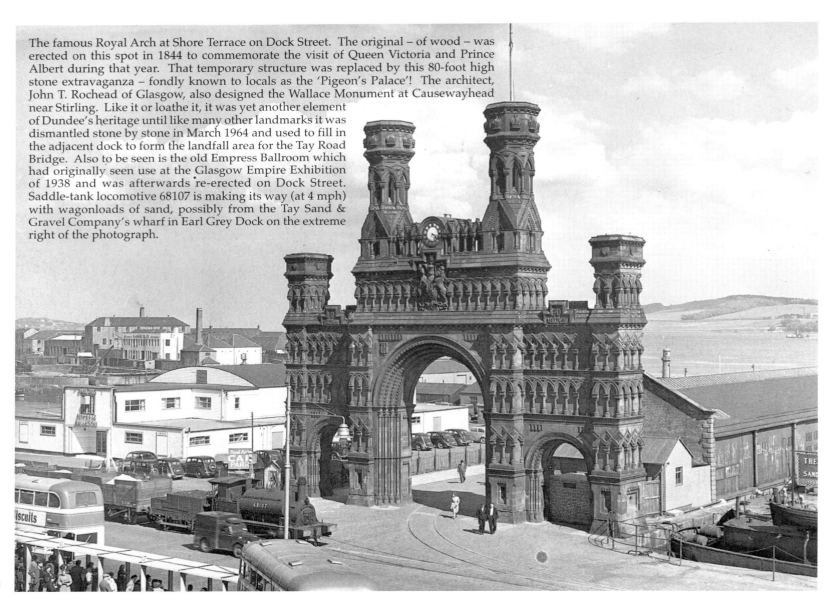

In the 1920s road-making was not highly mechanised. Here work is being undertaken on the extension of Dudhope Terrace at Inverlaw Place (on the right) through to Lochee Road. Dudhope House can be discerned through the trees on the right. This was built in 1850 for Mr Gardner of Dudhope on the site of a much earlier building. For over 30 years until 1969 it was used as a nurses' home for the Royal Infirmary, and thereafter became health board offices. It is now used as Tayside Primary Care NHS Trust's Centre for Child Health. This road extension may have attracted an Unemployment Alleviation Grant – many such improvement schemes of this period were so funded. The steam road roller on the left was owned by the Corporation, as was the Leyland lorry.

A blue solid-wheeled Fordson tractor seen on Dryburgh Farm in the early 1920s. Owned by the Scott's of Dundee's jute aristocracy, the farm was soon to be sold to the Corporation and built over for council housing. These tractors are remembered mostly for their fuel eccentricities – they were started on petrol, but when warmed up were switched over to TVO or Tractor Vaporising Oil, which was a mixture of petrol and paraffin usually in the proportion of 1:3 or 1:5. They are also recalled with little affection for their extreme difficulty in responding on a cold (usually both dark and wet) winter morning – when it would be necessary to take out the plugs and heat them by dousing them in petrol and setting them alight! The starting handle could inflict a vicious kickback and had to be swung with extreme care. The tractor has no mudguards – they came later, and the solid metal wheels with 'spuds' for increased grip meant that vehicles such as this were banned from public roads. Attached is a spring-toothed grubber for breaking up topsoil. The latest in mechanical aids when it was photographed, it is a far cry from today's totally enclosed, air-conditioned, stereo sound system fitted behemoths of the field, but was nevertheless a vast change from the preceding horse-powered appliance.

A thirties view looking up Crichton Street towards the High Street. To the right is the bright, clean stone of the newly completed City Square buildings (described by one architect as 'Stalinist architecture at its worst') with the inset entrance to the shops built into the basement. Round the corner was the entrance to the fruit and vegetable market, now long gone. Painted in a bright yellow livery, Corporation dustcart No. 4, registration TS 7530, was of 1928 vintage and had a long life. Specialised SD vehicles like this one were built by Shelvoke & Drewery Ltd. of Letchworth, Hertfordshire from 1923. Many were originally battery-operated with a speed controller very like that of a tramcar. The distant bus is TS 8420, a 1930 Leyland LT1, fleet number 28.

A Dundee Eastern Co-operative Society bread van decorated for a special occasion. The society was founded in 1873 and was known to generations of Dundonians as the 'Sosh'. This is said to have come about as a result of the letters SOSH being rubber-stamped after the signature of the applicant on the society's membership forms. The letters stood for 'signature of share holder', but the story may be apocryphal! To join members had to agree to take out twelve shares of a value of £1, plus pay a 1s. 3d. entrance fee. Groceries or other goods were paid up weekly and profits accrued distributed twice-yearly. At 68–72 Seagate the Sosh had its clothing, house-furnishing and other associated departments and made the following suggestion: 'Members wishing the best attention are strongly advised to shop early, and so avoid the crush in the evenings and on Saturday afternoons'. Forty branches were to be found throughout the city and suburbs with the regular dividends sometimes reaching as much as 3s. 8d. in the pound. In 1931 the 20,000 members generated a turnover of no less than £1¼ million. The coming of supermarkets saw the contraction, but not extinction, of the national co-op movement.

Four-wheeled carriers' carts such as this one were frequently to be seen around the city until the 1960s, and were commonly used for transporting goods to and from the railway stations. Businesses hung a card in the window reading 'Carriers cart today' to indicate to the carters that they required goods uplifted. Railways were of course the main carrier for virtually all goods over longer distances until the rise of the long-distance motor lorry transport industry, which became viable following the release of vast numbers of ex-army vehicles after World War I. Thereafter government investment in roads increased to the extent that only now do we appreciate the parlous state that the rail industry has been left in after generations of minimal investment. This LMS cart was photographed at Dundee West goods depot, with, naturally, a fine soft bundle for the drayman to perch on. Note also the wooden tea chests – invaluable for house removals – usually complete with tea dust in the corners and the associated aroma! In years gone by enamelled metal advertising signs such as these ones were fixed on every possible vertical surface.

David Barrie of Exchange Street was the owner of this solid-tyred lorry, supplied by Dennis Bros. of Guildford. It is seen here opposite his premises well-loaded with sacks, possibly containing flour imported through the docks. Standing to the right of the truck is John N. Watson, a director of the company, which grew through time to offer a freight service to London using AEC vehicles. The tenement at 7 Exchange Street behind is advertising apartments which were owned by a Mrs McNab. Even when this photograph was taken Exchange Street had a reputation as somewhere that changed its persona when day became night, with characters personified by 'Sophie' making it their haunt. Its closeness to the docks ensured that it was never a quiet 'backwater'.

The firm of Whyte Brothers of Stannergate was yet another local haulage contractor which expanded from small beginnings into long-distance operations. This Albion flatbed (a former bus) was photographed in Glasgow having uplifted a well-stacked payload of 'Uveco – the original flaked maize' (at least that is what is stencilled on the sacks). Probably imported into Glasgow from North America, maize is now the most widely grown crop in the world, but was then likely to have been used in this country as cattle feed (corn-on-the-cob was not then a delicacy on this side of the Atlantic). Having started life as a motorbus in Aberdeenshire, the vehicle illustrated here had an interesting history. W. Alexander & Co., motorbus proprietors, acquired it when they bought out its original owners, and it was purchased by Whyte's in 1939, lasting with them until 1942.

A model 'T' Ford from the parcels delivery department of the Dundee & District Mechanical Transport Service Co. The head office of this company was at a garage in Westfield Avenue off Perth Road, with the parcels delivery side more conveniently located in the city centre at Castle Street. Founded by William Burke, the company was among the pioneers of regular bus operations from Dundee to Forfar. It was purchased in July 1920 by the Scottish Motor Traction Company of Edinburgh along with four Thornycroft buses. The SMT Co. continued to operate services around the city until the end of 1949, when a rationalisation saw the routes, vehicles and garage premises handed over to W. Alexander Ltd. of Falkirk.

Dundee's first AA patrolman cut a dashing figure on his bicycle, complete with acetylene headlamp but without gears! Perhaps his most important function was to warn members of police activity on speed checks in the days before giving such warnings was banned. He was not well-equipped to handle breakdowns, the tiny tool bag suspended from his saddle barely large enough to contain a single spanner. The first patrolmen were introduced not long after foundation of the AA in 1905, but they are better remembered for their yellow and black motorcycles and sidecars – from which basic repairs were seemingly always possible – rather than their push-bikes. This photograph was taken in Dalkeith Road, looking north up the hill from Arbroath Road prior to construction of either the bowling green or tennis courts which came to occupy the site just beyond the house to the right. The tennis club is now called Craigmuir after the amalgamation of the original club, Craigielea, with Stobsmuir tennis club (which was situated next to Maryfield tram depot).

Baxter Park – where the tram in the picture on page 20 is heading – was the 36-acre gift to the citizens of Dundee of 'Jute Baron' Sir David Baxter and his sisters in 1863. It cost its donors £40,000, an immense sum then, and in addition a further £10,000 was put aside as a fund for maintenance in perpetuity. The grateful inhabitants thereupon raised the money to have a marble statue of Sir David placed in the grounds. However, this became subject to vandalism and was removed to the safer, if less appropriate, Albert Institute. The grounds were designed by Sir Joseph Paxton, considered by some to be best park designer of the Victorian era, and after completion passed into the care of the council. Baxter had opened his Lower Dens Jute Works in 1822 and the company expanded to such an extent that by the end of the nineteenth century it employed over 4,000 souls. In the mid-1920s it became part of the Low & Bonar group. This delightful scene of a concert party of Pierrots performing in the park, with stylish perambulators in the foreground, was probably taken in the summer of 1911. Recently the park has been the recipient of major cash grants from the Heritage Lottery Fund and Historic Scotland which should see it returned to its former glory. A community centre, function suite and cafe will be situated in the refurbished main pavilion.

Dundee fire brigade had a very responsible and hazardous role, having to deal with not infrequent conflagrations in the city's jute warehouses. One of the city's most serious fires took place at Watson's Bond on 9 July 1906. Thousands of spectators gathered to watch the total destruction of the city's largest whisky bond, and memories of rivers of blue-flamed whisky flowing into street drains proved as difficult to extinguish as the whisky itself! It was calculated that the quantity of spirit destroyed would have been sufficient to provide every man then living in Scotland with six bottles of whisky. A regular brigade had been formed as far back as 1835. Prior to that there were only privately-funded firefighters, provided either by individual insurance companies or mill owners. The initiative to form a public brigade was taken only after a disastrous fire in a Dock Street warehouse which resulted in five firefighters losing their lives under a falling gable. The brigade shown here comprised a complement of twenty men. With Captain James Weir, Dundee's firemaster from 1903-37 in front.

Mechanisation of the fire brigade led to the acquisition of this Merryweather fire tender, TS 1029, in 1917. It was photographed in front of the West Bell Street frontage of the Sheriff Court, just across the street from the central fire station, on 20 July of that year (the date is conveniently scratched on the negative). Initially the tender was used to haul 50 foot wheeled escape ladder which had previously been horse-drawn. The Sheriff Court building dates from 1833–34 and has been described by Professor Charles McKean as 'not untypical of a mid [nineteenth] century Edinburgh bank'. It nevertheless remains one of the city's more imposing frontages today.

Clepington Road in 1913, looking east from Fairmuir towards the top of Provost Road. Of particular interest is one of Dundee's two pioneering trolley buses – called 'Stouries' in the local vernacular after the clouds of dust that rose behind them in dry weather from the non-asphalted road surface. Complaints from the Highways Department about damage to the roads, and perhaps more importantly the consequent argument as to who was to pay to repair this, led to the trolley buses' abandonment in May 1914. The short 1¼ mile route ran only between Strathmartine Road and Forfar Road and the opening in September 1912 coincided with the meeting in the city of the British Association for the Advancement of Science. Two overhead wires were required, the second one to carry the electrical return. Electric trams used the rails to achieve this, but with the insulation of solid rubber tyres the trolley buses needed a different solution. Both vehicles (they were known as 'cars' and were numbered in the tram fleet) had 28-seat bodies and were supplied by the Railless Electric Traction Co. of London. After use in Dundee they were sold to Halifax Corporation where they saw limited further use.

The normal terminus for the Constitution Road ('Conshie') trams was the top of the Hilltown, by the clock, although for some time they ran through to Fairmuir and even to Downfield after 1922. The first regular Corporation bus service also passed this spot, and in this photograph a single deck Leyland PLSC1 (registration number TS 6993, fleet number 13, new in January 1928) is about to turn on to Mains Road. The tram rails leading off down Hilltown still remain, although the overhead wires have already been removed. As the Hilltown trams stopped running at the end of February 1928, the photograph was probably taken in the summer of that year. The white stripe on the pole to the left advised tram drivers that this was a 'feeder' where there was a power input to the overhead, requiring them to shut off the tram's controller as they passed under. The 'Conshie' cars were not worn out when they were withdrawn after 26 years in service on these steep hills; in contrast the replacement buses lasted just nine years!

Looking up Sandeman Street with Dens Park football ground to the right. The occasion is the still-remembered game of 3 January 1949 when the ground – packed with a 43,000-capacity record crowd – witnessed an historic 3–1 win against Glasgow Rangers by the local team, which had only that season returned to the first division. Entrance to the ground cost 1s. 9d. and on this particular occasion all Dundee supporters viewed this as a great investment! Despite the nature of the occasion there does not seem to be a single rosette or supporter's scarf in evidence – a great contrast to today's scene, where not to wear your team's colours is to invite 'comment'! Note also the emphatic signals of the two police officers to the driver of the saloon – not this way . . .

A special tram track looped round the Albert Institute taking 'Football Special' trams from Panmure Street back round to Meadowside, providing a constant stream of non-stop transport up Victoria Road and Dens Road to another special siding laid up Provost Road. This could hold up to twelve tramcars for returning fans. Car 54 was the second of several to be built in the Corporation Tramway workshops in Lochee Road during 1923–24. When this photograph was taken the trams had only a couple of years of life left, but standards were not allowed to slip and although some of the former elaborate gold lining is no longer in evidence, the tram has been turned out in pristine condition. On the right the inspector surveys the scene with the tram crew, wearing Dundee-style soft caps, keeping a watchful distance.

'Lochee' tram 19 heads into town along Ward Road with Guthrie Street leading off to Brook Street in the background between two of the city's imposing Victorian jute mill buildings. To the left is the much more modern frontage of St Roque's Automobile Co. Bearing up behind the tram is 'Utility' type Bedford bus YJ 8114 arriving at the Courthouse Square terminus of the service from Liff. Trams such as the one pictured here were the last obtained by Dundee City Tramways, with number 19 arriving in October 1930. With upholstered seats both in the lower saloon and upstairs they represented a great improvement over their predecessors. Intended for the Maryfield to Ninewells service, they were found to be too wide to pass each other on many parts of that line. Rather than reconstruct the tracks they were sent off to be appreciated by the inhabitants of the 'Dark Suburb'. A late-night trip down the steep route into town on the last car was not for the faint hearted!

An archetypal Dundee street scene of the 1950s, looking down the Cowgate with St Andrew Street off to the right and a tram coasting downhill from Maryfield arriving from King Street. The horse-drawn cart has a good load of jute sacking. A period flavour is added by the seemingly timeless advertisements on the facing gable featuring Ovaltine, Player's, Andrew's Liver Salts, and for added impact *two* posters exhorting readers to 'Join the Co-op and save as you spend'. Just before the abandonment of the trams in September 1956, this was the scene of one of Dundee's most spectacular tram incidents – which very fortuitously was without injury.

For some reason, in Albert Street at Arthurstone Terrace, both the driver and conductor left their vehicle to inspect a van parked too close to the track which had been given a 'nudge' by the tram, and in their absence it set off on its own down the steep hill! Careering through the Arbroath Road traffic lights it kept on the rails round the bend at the foot of Dens Brae, accelerated down King Street but was slowed outside the King's Cinema when it hit a lorry with a glancing blow. Crewless still, it took the bend into Murraygate before rolling to a halt – still on the rails – outside Smith Brothers' shop. Despite Dundee's many hills, this is one of the few occasions when any accident of this nature interrupted an impressive record of safe operation.

In the late summer of 1955, to assist in tram replacement (which was completed on 20 October 1956), the Transport Department purchased ten of these former London Transport AEC Regent II (STL type) buses which had already seen about ten years' use in the capital city. Nearest the camera is HGC 223, the name of its previous owners painted over, but still showing 'Hertford' as its destination. As Dundee Corporation No. 174 it saw another nine years' use before going for scrap in 1964.

One could be forgiven for thinking that this is Maryfield *Bus* Garage, but it is actually still Maryfield Tram Depot, albeit in the month prior to the abandonment of the trams. The original redbrick building dated from 1901 but was extended twice thereafter. Remarkably, after having been given up as a bus garage and having been used for several years by the City Parks Department, the building still exists, and even more remarkably there are still lengths of tram rail to be seen. The former London bus seen in the previous picture appears again here, on the right, heading for the city centre to go into service on route 1 to Beechwood. About to enter the depot is HGC 218 (No. 171) giving a rear view of the same ex-London type. Arranged outside the building are older Daimler vehicles – in the centre YJ 7054 of 1939 – and on the right an even older model which was to see just a few more months of service.

Perhaps second-only to Boots Corner at the foot of Reform Street as a trysting place was Wilson's Corner on Commercial Street – faced by another Dundee institution – D. M. Brown on the High Street corner opposite. Reference has been made earlier to criticism of Commercial Street's massive elevation, but this writer at least finds it a harmonious composition, functional but far from boring. This scene from the mid-1950s encompasses some typical Dundee 'wheels' – the tram heading for Downfield, the inward buses making for the Shore Terrace terminus, and the two Alexander's single-deckers heading out of town. In addition to these there is a single motor car and a horse and cart behind the tram, probably heading for the docks. Frequently cursed as an obstruction and delay to other road users, horse-drawn carts acted as the 'traffic calming' measures of 50 years ago. This picture also provides an opportunity to admire the fashions of the day, from headscarf to fur collar!

Baillie A. G. Hossick (deputising for the Lord Provost) on the saluting base in Panmure Street in front of the Queen Victoria statue at the Albert Institute, taking the salute at the parade held on 2 June 1953 to commemorate the Coronation of Queen Elizabeth. The 1,000-strong parade was just a part of Dundee's celebrations which also included a decorated tram and bus. The main part of the parade, which was led by 'Dundee's Own' – the 4th/5th Black Watch – consisted of local Territorials plus Auxiliaries, Home Guard and Cadets. Accompanying Baillie Hossick on the podium are Captain W. F. Keay RNVR, Brigadier J. A. Oliver and Wing Commander Ian McT. Ramsay. With their weapons in the dipped 'salute' are the smart Daimler armoured cars of 237–277 Field Squadron (Fife and Forfar Yeomanry TA). Three pipe bands accompanied the parade, which assembled at Riverside Drive and marched through the city along High Street, Reform Street, Panmure Street and Commercial Street to the East station. It was said that there would have been more spectators but many were still celebrating, glued to the latest innovation, television. TV sets were still a relative rarity (but the Coronation boosted sales enormously) and those fortunate few who owned one mostly had a full house of friends and neighbours.

The Tay Road Bridge was completed by Duncan Logan Ltd. (remember Loganair?) and was formally opened on 18 August 1966 by HM The Queen Mother. This view of the south end approach roundabout was taken very soon after and shows an Alexander (Fife) Ltd. double deck bus about to make the crossing. It also shows the concrete column which serves as a memorial to the workers who lost their lives during the construction period. The best appreciation of the actual shape of the bridge columns can be obtained from this roundabout. The height of the bridge reduces from the south side to the Dundee landfall, creating a very peculiar perspective. In June 1949 the 'Tay Valley Plan' stated: 'this report will produce facts which, if fully appreciated, will have the effect of bringing the Tay Road Bridge, if not an equal priority with the Forth Road Bridge because of the limitation of labour and material, to second priority to proceed immediately the Forth Bridge is completed', and noted that in twelve years usage of the Tay ferries had increased by 41 percent. (The equivalent figure for the Queensferry passage was 72 percent.) The report went on to reveal 'the urgent necessity for the bridge for economic and social development' and proposed a route for it to the *west* of the rail bridge. Unfortunately the powers that be within the city considered that this would lead to loss of trade and so the landfall was designed straight to the centre of the city at Shore Terrace – a monumental blunder which is now being reconsidered with a redesign of the north end of the bridge under contemplation. The far-sighted report also propounded that no branch railways or small stations be closed 'until it is certain that they will not be needed at some future date' – and that cheap hydroelectric power be used to electrify railways – particularly in the Highlands. This was a highly laudable and sensible proposal which could have revolutionised rail transport in east and central Scotland.